Chinese Fairy Tales

Translated by
Marie Ponsot

Illustrated by
Serge Rizzato

Ideals Publishing
Nashville, Tennessee

0-8249-8159-6

Contents

The Tortoise Prince 9

Green Chrysanthemums 15

The Queen of Tung Ting Lake 27

The Crystal Football 39

Huang and the Thunder Genie 45

Tao's Dream 51

The Extraordinary Beggar 57

THE TORTOISE PRINCE

Young Feng was too good-hearted. All his friends said so. Unfortunately, many of his friends took advantage of his kindness. They borrowed his money and never paid it back. Soon Feng had nothing left to lend. Indeed, he had nothing left at all.

One man, just one, tried to repay him. This was a poor fisherman. Since the fisherman had no money, he tried to pay his debt by sending Feng every tortoise he happened to catch in his net.

One day, the tortoise he sent was most unusual. It was very large and had a white mark on its head.

"I have never seen such a wonderful tortoise!" Feng said to himself. "It is as handsome as a work of art. It would be wrong to eat this rare creature," he thought. He gave the tortoise its freedom and did without supper that night.

One evening, months later, Feng was walking home along the river on a foot-path so narrow it could hold only one person at a time.

All of a sudden, he saw a dignified gentleman approaching, attended by four young servants.

"Can't you see I want to pass? Step down!" the gentleman demanded haughtily.

"I can't," replied Feng reasonably. "Your extreme rudeness won't let me."

The gentleman shouted furiously at his servants, "Seize this obstinate young man and beat him properly! Find out his name, and I shall file a complaint."

"Call back your servants sir, or I promise you, you will regret it," said Feng angrily. "I am not a dog, to be beaten at your pleasure. Feng is my name."

As soon as the gentleman heard the name of Feng his great fury turned into great joy. He knelt in the muddy path and bowed low, joyously crying, "You are the man who saved my life! I beg you to forgive me for what happened. Please do me the honor of coming with me and letting me explain."

Feng did not understand the gentleman's sudden change of heart. He forgave the rudeness but wanted no explanations. For he had no liking for changeable characters. But although he protested, the changeable gentleman took him firmly by the hand and led him quickly along, smilingly deaf to his objections.

Before long, they came to the gentleman's house, which Feng found very beautiful. It had broad, cool porches and restful, richly furnished rooms.

Finally, the unknown gentleman sat down and said, "Welcome, Feng. You are by far the most welcome of any guest I can imagine. I am the eighth Prince of Tiao River. I was coming back from a garden party on the western hill when we met just now. I was fleeing the ugly, illiterate snobs who posed in front of the beautiful flowers at this party. The rage they caused me exploded most wrongly on you. Do forgive me, I beg you."

Feng realized his host was a genie. Only a silly man takes offense at a genie's manners. Besides, the nice way the genie was treating him now put him at his ease. Feng decided to enjoy himself. Servants soon set a wonderful dinner before them. They ate and talked, and the time passed quickly.

At last, a bell sounded in the distance. The prince got up and took Feng by the arm. "You are good company," he said. "But I am sorry to say that we will have to leave each other for the bell has summoned me away. Allow me to give you something you may find useful. You will not be able to keep it forever, but I will not come to take it back until your every wish is fulfilled."

Smiling benevolently, he pinched Feng's arm with so mighty a pinch that

Feng cried out and tears sprang to his eyes. "There you are, dear friend, and now you may leave," said the prince. Then he saw Feng out with a bow of profound respect.

As he walked away, Feng took a look at his arm. Neat and clear as a tattoo, just where the prince had pinched him was a perfect thumb-sized image of a tortoise with a white mark on his head.

That was surprising, but only half as surprising as what happened when Feng looked down at the ground he stood upon. The earth had become as transparent as crystal to his eyes. And under about a foot of earth, at his feet, he could see a huge pearl.

Feng knelt and dug. After digging for awhile, he reached the pearl and found that it was real. Feng looked around him in wonderment. The earth no longer hid its treasures, but disclosed them plainly to his sight. Wherever he looked on the ground, he saw jewels and other precious objects.

Right then and there, he promised himself that he would put the prince's fine parting gift to some sort of good use. Then he continued home in excellent spirits.

When Feng got back to his dilapidated old house, the first thing he saw was a large pile of silver buried beneath it. He dug it out, and was poor no more. Soon after, he heard that there was another rickety wreck of a house for sale. He went to look at it, and saw another pile of silver buried under the chimney. After he made this discovery, he bought the place at once.

In no time at all Feng became enormously rich. Jewels and precious stones of all colors and sizes filled the rooms of his many houses.

As he walked one day on the grounds of his summer house, Feng discovered a remarkable mirror which had a design in beaten gold and silver on the back of it. The glass in this mirror did not show the person who stood before it. Instead, on its clear surface it showed the image of whatever truly beautiful girl it had last reflected. The image remained until a still more beautiful girl passed before it.

Feng experimented a little and proved that the mirror really worked, even at a distance. It became the most precious of his possessions and he allowed no one to touch it.

One day, news came to Feng's village that the third daughter of Prince Su, the marvelously beautiful Lotus Crown, planned to visit a pool in the neighboring hills. The pool was famous for the quality of its spring water.

Hearing this news, Feng packed his magic mirror in a protective covering and left for the hills at once. When he came to the pool, he hid himself behind a rock above it, made himself comfortable, and sat down to wait.

The royal procession arrived. The porters, carrying the princess' canopied sedan chair, halted just below the rock behind which Feng was hidden. The curtains were drawn aside and in all her beauty, lighter than a feather, Lotus Crown stepped out.

For an instant the hidden mirror reflected her smiling face. Feng put the mirror back in its protective cover, and taking great care not to be seen, he returned home.

At home, he put the mirror on a small table. When he uncovered it, he gasped at the beauty of the face that smiled at him from the glass. The image was so true he half expected it to speak, and he half hoped the lowered eyes would lift to look into his.

With a sigh, Feng covered the mirror and hid it well. It would have been joy to gaze endlessly on that faultless face, but Feng was prudent. He allotted himself one hour a day before the mirror to gaze at the princess. At those times he made absolutely sure he was alone.

Yet somehow the word got around that young Feng had fallen utterly in love with the third daughter of Prince Su, Lotus Crown, whose portrait he kept hidden in his room. Finally, the rumor reached the prince's palace and finally, the prince himself heard about it and flew into a rage. He ordered the mirror to be taken and Feng to be brought before him.

"You have dared to look upon my daughter. You are too bold. Tomorrow at dawn your guilty head will be cut off," announced the prince.

Feng replied with dignified calm, "I am guilty. I cannot undo my bold crime, or even regret it. You cannot pardon it. Yet, my lord, consider one other thing: I have a rare gift. I can find the most precious things on earth, no matter how or where they lie hidden. Should you cut off my head, a process of no profit to anyone, the gift would be lost. Spare me, and my gift will provide infinite riches for your pleasure."

"Nonsense," said the prince. "I don't believe one word. You die at dawn."

Feng was hustled off to jail to await his death. Prince Su went to his rooms to recover from his rage. There he found his third daughter, Lotus Crown, waiting

for him. She was the favorite of all his children, and he had no wish to hurt her.

Softly she said, "Father, I have been seen by this Feng. Killing him fifty times won't change that fact. Only one thing can restore my honor. I must marry Feng."

"Never. I forbid it," Prince Su replied.

"Very well. Then honor demands that I die. I shall starve myself," said the beautiful princess in tears.

Prince Su was sure that this was only an idle threat. But just in case she had meant it, he sent word that Feng's execution would be postponed for another three days.

Once an hour during those days he sent for news of his daughter. The news was always the same; she would not eat.

Finally, more enraged than ever, the prince ordered that Feng the prisoner become Feng the free. And he announced the engagement of Feng and Lotus Crown.

As soon as he was set free, Feng ran home to prepare Princess Lotus Crown's engagement presents. A thousand richly uniformed servants, each bearing a great golden vase packed with precious gems, presented themselves and their priceless burdens to Prince Su, as a token of Feng's respect.

Su had to admit that his prospective son-in-law had good qualities as well as bad. He scarcely regretted having let Feng keep his head.

Blessed with happiness, Feng and his royal bride set up housekeeping in a magnificent pavilion. In the place of honor stood the famous mirror, which from then on faithfully reflected the radiant image of Lotus Crown, the mistress of the house.

Feng, alone in his room one evening, turned to see the eighth Prince of Tiao River come in. Bowing, Feng welcomed him and invited him to sit down. The river prince said, "I regret that once more I have very little time. I have come for the gift I gave you. You do not need it, since you will never lack for anything again."

Smiling, he pinched Feng's arm with a mighty pinch. Feng's eyes blurred with pain. By the time he could see again, Prince Tiao had gone. He drew up his silken sleeve, and saw that the mark of the tortoise had disappeared too.

Anxious to thank Prince Tiao again, Feng hurried out. There was no one in sight. There was only a very large tortoise. It trundled patiently down to the river, plunged in, and was seen no more.

14

GREEN CHRYSANTHEMUMS

Wen was born loving music. He made it his chief study for many years, until he became a lutist of great skill.

Wherever he went, Wen took his lute. Whenever he had a free hour, he played to perfect his touch on the instrument.

One evening, late, he was on his way home. The sun had set while he still had far to go. It began to rain. Wen quickened his pace and looked for shelter. When he came to a village along the road, he entered the first gate he saw. The house appeared uninhabited, but Wen didn't mind so long as he had a roof for the night. He crossed the courtyard and went into a room that was completely empty.

Suddenly the door opened and a pretty young girl entered. She took one look at Wen and fled.

Before he had any time to think, the door opened again, and an old woman came in. "Who are you?" she demanded of Wen. "And how, may I ask, did you get in?"

Bowing, he replied politely, "Wen is my name. I was on my way home, and I turned in here seeking shelter from the rain. Would you please allow me to stay until morning?"

"You are welcome to stay," the woman said. "But we have little to offer, not even a bed. Since you are young and healthy, you should be able to make do with an armful of straw."

"Gladly," Wen said.

The old woman went out and brought back a lamp. In a corner she scattered a little straw. She seemed a simple, kindly person. Wen could not resist saying, "A beautiful young lady came in here before. Please, can you tell me who she is?"

"That was my niece, Fragrant Flower."

"May I see her again—just for a moment?"

"I'm afraid that is out of the question," the old woman answered.

With these words, she went out. Wen saw that the straw was sparse as well as damp and old. He decided to forego sleep for that night. Fortunately he had with him the means to enjoy himself. His back against the wall, he sat down to play the lute.

On the stones of the courtyard, on the tiles of the roof, the rain kept up its unfaltering rhythm. Wen tempered his lute music to the murmur of the rain and began to compose a very gentle song, telling of the sadness of the end of summer, the gaiety of the beginning of autumn.

The door opened quietly, and the pretty girl slipped into the room. Wen rose and bowed, but the girl said, "Please, please don't stop playing. I'll go. Mayn't I hear that song once more?"

"With pleasure," Wen said. He plucked the lute strings and sang, "The green wood now grows gray, alas." Fragrant Flower listened, and when he had done she pleaded, "Won't you show me how the lute is played?"

Wen was glad to share his enthusiasm with someone. He spent the long hours of the night teaching Fragrant Flower to play the lute. She learned quickly, and by dawn she could play two or three simple songs.

Although he had not slept a wink, Wen did not feel at all tired after a night spent so pleasantly. But the rain had stopped, and he had no further reason to stay in the house. Before going, he asked the old woman if he might return to visit her lovely niece.

"No, young man. Your influence is not desirable. Fragrant Flower stayed up all

16

night to learn music with you. It was a serious breach of good manners. And it is something which I cannot allow."

Without another word, she took the girl by the hand and led her away. Wen did not even have a chance to say good-bye. Astonished, he waited a few moments, then went out into the courtyard. He looked back at the house. It seemed deserted. No sign of life came from within. All the way home Wen wondered about his strange adventure.

The wealthy Lord Koo often invited Wen to his handsome residence to play the lute. More than once Wen, as he played, had seen a bamboo curtain drawn aside to reveal the delicate face of a young girl. He had learned that it was Koo's daughter, First Rose.

17

One day Wen said, "Mother, I would like you to ask my Lord Koo's permission for me to marry his daughter."

"Son, you are foolish to hope for it. Koo is enormously rich. You are only a poor lute player."

"Please try, at least," he insisted.

But his mother was right. Not only did Koo refuse the proposal, but also, thinking the young man quite impudent, he became very annoyed and stopped inviting him to his home.

But beautiful First Rose had fallen in love with Wen and his enchanting music. When she learned that he had wanted to marry her and that her father had refused the proposal, she wept and wept, and wrote woeful love poems, which she destroyed as soon as they were written.

Walking in her garden one day, First Rose noticed a scroll of paper lying among the sweet alyssum. She picked it up and saw that it bore a long poem written in green ink. The first verse began, "The green wood now grows gray, alas."

She thought it a lovely poem—even the loveliest she had ever read. Returning to her room, she made a copy of it on a sheet of her best paper and left it on her desk so that the ink would dry.

A few moments later, Koo came into her room. He happened to see the sheet of paper and leaned over to read it. " 'The woods grow gray,' " he muttered. "What nonsense girls write! It is high time First Rose had a husband." While saying this, he held the paper to the lamp and burned it, then tossed the ashes out of the window into the garden.

First Rose, finding the poem gone, thought the wind had carried it away and regretted her carelessness. Next day, sad and melancholy, she was strolling again in her garden. Suddenly she stopped, amazed, at the place where the evening before she had found the poem and where, by chance, the ashes scattered by Koo had fallen.

From the ashes had risen two magnificent chrysanthemums, tall and stately—and strange. For these were not white or gold or any ordinary color, but green, as green as the purest jade!

20

Every member of the household came to the garden to see the jade-green chrysanthemums, and news of this novelty spread quickly. The whole village heard of them, then the whole countryside.

Scientists, societies of artists, flower arrangers, groups of amateur growers, prominent horticulturists, and shrewd dealers in rarities came from far and near. Once they had seen the jade-green blossoms, each of them hoped for a cutting from the plants.

Soon Koo had to ask the governor for a military guard to keep strangers from pillaging his garden. He was so busy protecting his valuable green flowers that he had no time to think about a marriage for First Rose.

A few weeks later, another extraordinary thing happened. One beautiful morning, Wen went out to water his garden. He stared, shook his head, rubbed his eyes, and stared again. All his chrysanthemums had turned green—jade-green, jasper-green, brilliant as jewels.

Early the next day he went to the garden, almost expecting the chrysanthemums to have vanished or to have turned white and gold again. But they still stood, jade-green, jasper-green, astonishing. And between their stems was a scroll. Wen picked it up and read, in amazement, the verses of the song he had composed one happy, rainy night: "The green wood now grows gray, alas."

Lord Koo heard rumors of Wen's chrysanthemums, and decided to call on Wen that very day.

"I fail to understand why you should have green chrysanthemums, young man," said Koo. "Didn't you know that, until now, mine were unique, the only green chrysanthemums anywhere?"

"Nor do I understand it, my Lord Koo," said Wen. "Please do me the honor of entering my poor home. We may discuss our gardens there."

Koo could not refuse, and they went into Wen's house. Wen left for a moment to order refreshments, leaving the scroll bearing the poem on a table near the door. Koo, who was naturally curious and had small respect for the privacy of this impudent, young lute player, picked up the scroll and read it.

"Why, this is my daughter's poem!" he exclaimed. "How does Wen come to have it?"

Wen returned to be confronted by the angry father.

"Where did you get my daughter's poem?" Koo demanded.

Slowly Wen shook his head. "Your daughter's poem? I regret having to correct you, sir. But your daughter did not write those lines; I did. They are words for a song I wrote one rainy night not long ago."

"Then you sent it to First Rose, you sly, impudent whippersnapper!"

"No, my Lord. I swear it. I was surprised to find that scroll in the garden just this morning."

"I now begin to see how the green chrysanthemums have begun to grow in your garden. Obviously my daughter was foolish enough to send you both the poem and the plants!"

Fuming, deaf to reason, Koo stormed home and told his wife. She listened in silence. But, being a sensible woman, when he was through ranting and raving, she calmly reminded him, "We have no positive proof that First Rose sent Wen either the plants or the poem. Nor do we know he sent them to her. It would harm us all to make a scandalous affair out of this incident. I think I shall believe that the green chrysanthemums are a sign from the gods that our families should unite. Give First Rose in marriage to Wen, and let us say no more about it."

Her words were so gentle and wise that Koo admitted she must be right. He sent for Wen, and for his daughter, and told them of his decision. They were both over-joyed, and wedding preparations were begun at once.

That night Wen could not sleep at all. He stayed up till dawn, playing the lute and singing with his friends out in the garden, within sight of the jade-green flowers.

The marriage of Wen, a poor lute player, to First Rose, daughter of the wealthy Lord Koo, was joyously celebrated.

One rainy evening, the young couple sat talking, when First Rose tilted her head and said, "Listen!"

They heard strange, soft music which seemed to be coming from the next room.

"Someone is playing your lute," said First Rose.

"That's odd," replied Wen. "I'll go and see who it is."

Wen went out and came back carrying his lute. He frowned and said, "There was no one there."

"But your lute cannot play by itself," said his wife.

He set the instrument on a cushion and moved away a few steps. All at once the strings of the lute began to vibrate, and their sweet sound could be heard. Yet there was still no player to be seen.

First Rose shivered. "It can be only magic," she said. "What are we to do?"

Wen was not sure. This was so strange a thing—his own lute played by invisible fingers! He was frightened, but not wishing to appear a coward or to offend whatever spirit was visiting his house, he said, very humbly, "Genie or fairy, your Excellence, whoever you may be, will you not free my wife of fear and say what you want of us?"

A gay laugh mingled with the music. The lights flickered, and a beautiful girl appeared before the astonished couple. She held the lute in her arms and gently plucked the strings.

"Who are you?" asked First Rose.

"Fragrant Flower!" Wen exclaimed at the same time.

"Yes, it is I, Fragrant Flower," said the girl. "I have come to see if you wish to thank me for what I have done for you."

First Rose felt an immediate liking for the merry, innocent maiden. "We wish to do whatever you wish us to do," she said. Looking at Wen, she saw that he agreed.

"That is kind," Fragrant Flower said. "I wish, please, to have you think of me as kindly as I think of you. It was I who arranged your marriage. I planted the jade-green, jasper-green chrysanthemums. I made you each a scroll bearing the poem. It seemed the best way to prove my gratitude to Wen, who is a most skilled and most gentle music teacher."

"Does your aunt know of all this?" Wen asked.

"That poor good soul whom you met was not my aunt, but a servant of my father's. He is a very powerful genie. I had been disobedient, and would not study, you see. My father was very angry with me. My punishment was to spend every rainy night here on earth in an abandoned, miserably uncomfortable house. After you taught me to play the lute, my father put an end to the punishment. He was so pleased with my singing and playing that I have studied music ever since. So I wanted to show my thanks to my first teacher, who freed me from my father's disfavor and brought me such joy."

The young couple bowed deeply and said, "Fragrant Flower, please, let us persuade you to stay awhile with us. We can all share our music, and your company would be a delight."

"I regret to say that this is impossible," said the pretty girl. "I must hurry right

home as it is, or run the risk of another scolding from my father. Farewell to you both!"

And before either Wen or First Rose could say another word, she was gone. Wen took his lute and sang to his bride as he played, "The green wood now grows gray, alas." He sang these words of their lovesong with a great deal of vigor. And blushing, First Rose joined him in her delicate voice.

Neither Wen nor First Rose ever saw Fragrant Flower again. But they remained grateful to her all their happy lives. They thought of her each year when in Wen's small garden the famous jade-green, jasper-green chrysanthemums burst into brilliant bloom.

THE QUEEN OF TUNG TING LAKE

Chen was an ambitious young man with an eager and able mind. Since his family was too poor to make him a scholar, he became the secretary of a famous general who governed Pekin.

One day, Chen and the general were crossing Tung Ting Lake aboard a junk when a seal swam by. The general fitted an arrow to his bow and shot the seal, just to keep in practice.

The sailors hauled the creature aboard. As they tied it to the foot of the mast, they noticed a strange thing. A small fish had attached itself to the seal's tail. Even out of water it still held fast to the seal.

Pleased with himself, the general went to bed. Chen stayed on deck. The seal was still alive and gasping painfully.

Chen took out a healing powder he had compounded, and sprinkled some on the seal's back. Then he untied the suffering creature and tossed it into the water.

"Good! It will live," thought Chen. He watched the seal plunge joyfully, circling the junk. It was joined by a school of shining fishes, some of them resembling the one that had gripped the seal's tail so firmly.

The general didn't mind finding the seal gone. It was the shot, not the victim, that had pleased him. Chen, too, forgot about it.

A year later, on his first vacation, Chen crossed the lake to visit his family. A sudden tempest arose, and the junk was smashed to pieces. Chen clutched a bamboo basket and managed to stay afloat until he could grab the roots of a tree that grew on the bank.

Soaked and chilled, he waited for dawn. The lake shore was deserted and tempest-torn. Not a junk was in sight. A green hill sloped up from the shore, covered with graceful willow trees whose leaves trembled in the soft breeze.

Chen started to climb up the hill, hoping to find someone to tell him the way to his native village. He was about half way up, when suddenly an arrow whistled past his ear. Chen turned to see two maidens galloping by on swift horses.

Their heads were banded with red silk and their black hair streamed behind them. Their dresses were purple, belted in green, and they were armed with bows and arrows. Black leather quivers hung at their shoulders and bows were slung across their saddles.

Chen ducked hurriedly behind a tree, and waited until the horses were out of sight. Then he continued up the hill. When he reached the top, he saw many girls in identical hunting costumes. They were dancing and laughing, and playing hide-and-seek among the willows and the walnut trees. There were no men there, only a dozen small boys serving refreshments.

One of these boys passed near to where Chen stood out of sight, trying to get his bearings.

Chen stepped out and whispered,

"Where am I, for heaven's sake?"

The boy looked around and laughed.

"Don't you know? This is the hunting ground of the queen of Tung Ting Lake. How on earth did you get here?"

"The storm last night sank my junk. I barely escaped alive. Now I am hungry and thirsty, and lost besides."

"Hunger and thirst are easily satisfied," the boy said, offering Chen the picnic provisions he carried. "But if you value your life, get out of here before the queen sees you."

With that, he ran off to serve the maidens, who were still playing and dancing.

Chen circled to by-pass the dell, keeping well out of sight behind the trees. There was a path down the far slope, and Chen followed it until he came to a white wall that he supposed must enclose a temple. Around the wall ran a limpid brook, across which was a stone bridge that led to a door.

Trying to quiet his fears, Chen crossed the bridge and went through the door. He found himself in a vast park. Shrines rose here and there among the flowering trees and shrubs.

Chen wandered on through the stillness, and presently he came to a clearing ringed by weeping willows. A gentle breeze stirred the branches of the trees, and petals from the wisteria drifted down to the ground. Birds sang sweetly.

29

Chen stood still, enchanted. Such loveliness surpassed anything he had ever imagined. Then he noticed a swing in the clearing. Its ropes rose with no support into the sky, and vanished among silvery clouds.

Chen began to be afraid. The garden was too beautiful and too lonely. Chen wanted to leave. But the sound of laughter and light steps warned him that someone was approaching. He hurried into the dense shrubbery, and the girls he had seen earlier came into view, laughing and singing.

Soon another group of girls joined the first. Gowned in purple, they accompanied a princess of indescribable beauty.

They served her with a tea whose warm fragrance drifted over to Chen. He stood spellbound.

When she had finished the tea, she tossed back her black locks and ran joyously to the swing. Light as a summer swallow she soared, so high she became a silver blur among the clouds. The maids-in-waiting stood and watched her, applauding as the swing went higher. Down she came, and soared again, up, up, again and again, her long hair blowing around her face.

At last she grew tired of this pastime. She let the rhythm shorten, the maidens caught hold of the swing, and the princess stepped down.

The maids-in-waiting surrounded her, and they went off, laughing and chattering, through the flowering trees.

Chen stepped from his hiding place and approached the swing. The beauty of the princess had driven from his mind his urgent longing to escape.

On the grass near the swing lay a red silk kerchief. Chen picked it up and thrust it into his sleeve. Then he set off through the forest, following the path taken by the princess and her maidens.

He came to an archway inlaid with mother-of-pearl. It sheltered a table that bore materials for writing. Seized with inspiration, Chen took out the red silk kerchief, and began to write verses to the beautiful princess.

"Your black locks toss in the balmy air
Where you dart and fly on your graceful swing.
You dip and soar, more immortally fair
And more longed-for than spring."

The verses sang of the beauty of the princess in terms of such infinite sweetness, that were so full of emotion, that they seemed to be the work of a great poet.

Chen put the handkerchief back into his sleeve with a great sigh, and went to search for a way out of the royal grounds.

He tried to remember the way he had come in, but the longer he walked among the flowering trees and temples, the more lost he became.

Suddenly he emerged from a bower of vines and found himself face to face with one of the attendant maidens.

"Who are you? How did you get here?" she asked in astonishment.

Bowing, Chen replied,

"I wandered in here, looking for the way home to my village. Help me find a way out, I beg you."

"I too am looking for something lost. Have you seen a red silk kerchief anywhere?"

"Is this it?" Chen asked, drawing the kerchief from his sleeve.

"Oh, yes!" she cried. Then seeing it covered with writing, she shook it out and read the verses.

"Now I could not help you, even if I wanted to," she said sadly.

"Why not?" Chen asked.

"This is the princess' favorite kerchief. She wears it constantly. She will never forgive you for all this ink." The maiden looked up at Chen sadly. "It's a pity. You seem a pleasant person, and you write well. I should have liked to help."

The maiden ran off through the trees, leaving Chen confused and anxious.

She returned just as the sun was setting.

"I have good news," she said. "Her Highness read your verses. And instead of being annoyed, she was delighted! Be patient, and you may yet go free. But whatever you do, beware of climbing trees or walls. That would be unpardonable."

Again she left him, and disappeared among the foliage.

Chen waited, and shadows began to fill the little shrine. He dared not leave, for he was afraid the maiden might not be able to find him again.

Hours later, a small light came glimmering towards him. The maiden approached, followed by a servant bearing food and drink.

"I asked the princess if I might send you on your way," she said. "Her Highness felt it would be foolish for you to leave on a moonless night as dark as this one. She asked me to bring you these refreshments. So you see, all may yet be well."

But Chen was still troubled. He ate very little, and he could not sleep for puzzling over his strange captivity.

Next morning, the maiden came again, bringing him breakfast.

When Chen once more pleaded with her to help him escape, she murmured,

"Her Highness makes her own decisions. None of us would dare interfere."

Chen spent a long, anxious day. At sunset the maiden came running back.

"Something terrible has happened," she said breathlessly. "A gossipy girl has told the queen herself about the red kerchief, and the queen is furious. Now I am afraid for your safety!"

Chen was about to question her when they heard voices, and a party of men marched up. Carrying heavy chains in their hands, they surrounded Chen like a living wall, and their expressions were far from friendly. Behind them came several serving-maids.

One of them stepped forward and approached Chen. She stared closely at him, and cried,

"Incredible! It can't be, but it is! It is my lord Chen, indeed it is!"

She put herself between Chen and the men, who began to murmur among themselves. They moved closer to Chen, holding their chains in readiness.

"Wait!" cried the girl. "I must see the queen at once. Do nothing until I return."

Reluctantly the men stepped back. They stood quite still, gripping the chains in their powerful hands. The serving-maids whispered and stared. Chen spent a long moment of dread.

32

At last the maid came running back.

"Her Majesty the Queen asks my lord Chen to come to her at once!" she cried breathlessly.

Chen did not even try to understand the new turn of events. The men, their unused chains clanking, led him to a palace, through many rooms, and up to a pavilion. Its doors were hidden by a green bamboo curtain which hung from silver rings. A servant drew aside the curtain and announced,

"My lord Chen!"

Upon a gleaming throne of gold and silver sat a woman of great beauty. She was robed in brocade.

Chen knelt before her, and bowing low, he said,

"Your Majesty, I am a stranger who has come a long way. I beg you to set me free."

The queen rose and helped Chen to his feet. Gently she said, "My lord Chen, I owe you my life. Had my people known you, you would never have fared so badly in my realm. Can you forgive us?"

Before Chen could recover from his amazement, servants started to prepare a sumptuous banquet. Delicacies of every description were brought in on plates and bowls of pale, rosy porcelain so fine it seemed made of the sunlit petals of apple blossom.

The queen seated Chen beside her.

"It was good fortune that you found my daughter's kerchief. She will be honored to become your wife."

To Chen the news was amazing and wonderful. But since he could understand nothing of his extraordinary circumstances, he continued to feel anxious and uneasy.

When the banquet was over, a servant advised the queen,

"The princess is ready for the ceremony."

Chen followed the queen into a great hall. Thick, deep carpets covered the floors. Thousands of lanterns hung from the walls and ceilings. The air was sweet with soft music and the scent of musk.

The fair princess came modestly forward. She and Chen were married, and all the court held a festival.

The princess made a perfect wife.

Chen knew that he was most fortunate, and had every reason to rejoice. But until he could understand the reason for the queen's sudden kindness, he could not be at peace.

At last he decided to find out the truth, come what may. He said to his wife,

"I was nobody special. I was shipwrecked and lost. I found your kerchief and dared scrawl verses on it, and it almost cost me my life. Then all of a sudden I was showered with kindness, and given the greatest of gifts when you became my wife. To what do I owe this good fortune?"

The princess smiled and caressed his hand.

"Do you recall the day the general shot a seal as you were crossing Tung Ting Lake?" she said.

"I do. But how did you hear of it?" he exclaimed.

"The seal whose life you saved was one of the shapes sometimes taken by my mother, queen of the lake. We have never forgotten what we owe to your kindness."

"What about the serving-maid who recognized me? I had surely never seen her before."

"Perhaps you remember that a fish gripped the seal's tail and would not let go. That was the brave little maid who refused to abandon her queen. Of course she recognized you!"

At last Chen understood. Joy truly entered his heart. But he had one more question still to ask.

"When you saw your red kerchief scrawled with ink, you intended to have me put to death. Why did you keep putting it off? Why did you send a maid with food and drink?"

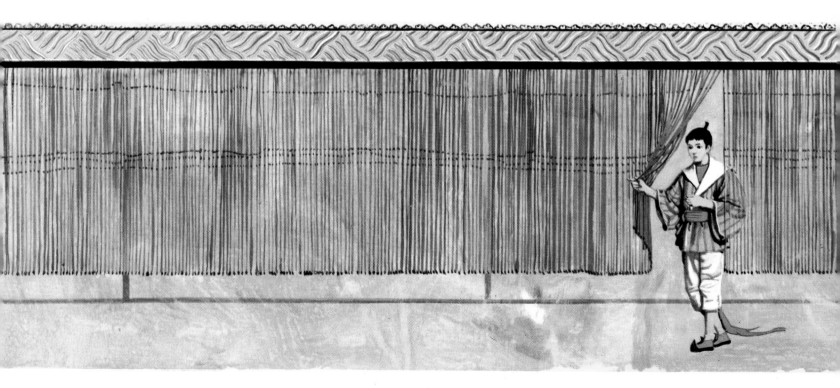

The princess turned her head aside and spoke very softly.

"When I read the poem I was filled with love for the one who wrote it. I hoped to find a way to soften my mother's heart toward him."

Chen sighed happily. He had no further questions to ask.

Ten years had passed since Chen's wedding to the princess of Tung Ting Lake. One night, the mandarin Liang was crossing the lake on his return from a long voyage in the south. Across the deep stillness, mingled with the murmur of the waters, he heard the sound of music.

Out of curiosity, Liang went on deck and saw a junk wreathed in flowers gliding toward him. Its wood was carved, and inlaid with pearl; its shutters were lacquered in scarlet. The deck was deserted, but from within came the sound of laughter and song.

The two boats were close together when he saw a shutter open. A beautiful young woman looked out over the water.

Behind her, a handsome young man sat at a festive table. Liang found the young man's face familiar. He thought for a moment, and then let out an exclamation of surprise.

"Chen!" he cried. "Chen, is that really you?"

Hearing his name, Chen ordered his junk to stop. He stared over the dark water to see who had hailed him. "Liang!" he called in pleased surprise. He had recognized the mandarin as his closest boyhood friend.

Liang accepted Chen's invitation to come aboard and be presented to his wife. He wondered how it was that Chen, the penniless student, was now Chen the wealthy husband of this most exquisite and elegant lady.

His wonder grew as servants cleared silver dishes away and brought others of wrought gold, studded with diamonds and full of delicious things to eat.

"Forgive an old friend's curiosity," he said at last. "When we last met ten years ago, you were less wealthy, were you not?"

Chen laughed and laughed.

"I was," he said. "I was poor as could be. Tell me, is this your first trip home since then?"

"Yes, I have spent the last ten years far to the south," Liang replied.

"Then that is why you haven't heard anything about me," Chen said, amused.

Liang felt rather awkward and ill-informed.

"May I ask where you and your lady are traveling?" he asked.

"We are just passing a few pleasant hours on the lake," Chen replied.

Liang nodded, and drank the rest of the wine in his cup before he rose to go.

"Let me offer you a little souvenir," Chen said. "It isn't often one meets an old friend after so many years."

He held out the largest pearl Liang had ever seen. Its perfect shape and its amazing luster were equally remarkable. Chen accompanied his friend on deck and waited until Liang stood safe on his own junk. Then he called for the sail to be hoisted. The night wind soon bore his flower-wreathed junk out of sight.

Two days later, Liang was home in his and Chen's native village. At the earliest opportunity he asked a friend,

"What news is there of my old friend Chen? All I know is that he is fabulously rich and has a most beautiful wife."

His friend stepped back and stared at him.

"Chen? If you mean Chen our schoolmate you've made a mistake. He was secretary to a general, years ago. He was crossing Tung Ting Lake to spend his first vacation here at home, and a storm sank his junk. Chen was drowned. They never even found his body. He's been dead for years."

Liang was too astonished to make any reply. Later he went to his room, opened his strong box and took out the pearl. It was real; it was there in his hand; it was the finest pearl he had ever seen.

Liang never found an explanation for his strange meeting with Chen. Nor did he ever sell the priceless pearl, which is still in the possession of his family. It passes from generation to generation, still holding its unfathomable secret.

THE CRYSTAL FOOTBALL

Wang and his father lived happily and peacefully by the shores of Grand Lake. They got along perfectly with one another for they had similar dispositions and the same tastes. Both were merry, brave, fond of good company, and marvelous football players.

One day tragic news came to Wang. His father had fallen from a junk while he was crossing the lake, and had drowned. Wang mourned deeply, for he had lost both his father and his dearest companion.

Eight years went by since the fatal accident. Wang had become a successful man of affairs. He often had to cross the lake on business. One beautiful night he was aboard his junk, anchored in the middle of the lake. The moon rose on the horizon, and its silver rays shined in Wang's calm eyes as he stood on deck watching.

As he looked along the ribbon of the moon's reflected light, he saw five men emerge from the water with a great roll of netting. They spread it out over the lake, stepping slowly and with ease on the surface of the water. As they set out refreshments in splendid array on the netting, three personages of obvious importance

39

rose from the water. One was dressed entirely in white; the other two were robed in yellow. All three wore curiously shaped hats that seemed black in the bright moonlight.

The five servants began to serve the three personages. They came and went, bearing goblets and dishes. One of these five was a young boy; three were strapping young men. As for the fifth, he was an older man, and Wang had a feeling that he knew him.

The personage dressed in white lifted his glass. It was full of a liquid that looked like melted silver. He said, "Tonight the moonlight is even more beautiful than usual."

"It is," one of the personages in yellow agreed. "It reminds me of the night the prince of the Emerald Isle gave his wonderful banquet."

"Forget the past. Think only of tonight," interrupted the third personage. "Drink up, and be gay."

The banquet proceeded, bathed in the clarity of the moonlight.

On Wang's junk the whole crew watched the spectacle. They lay on deck, not daring to make a move or to speak a word. The sailors were sure that the mysterious beings feasting on the surface of the water on the floating net were lake genies, and they were terrified.

Only Wang stood up and openly watched the banquet. He fixed his eyes on the scene with the utmost curiosity. The oldest servant looked so much like his father that he could not turn away. The more Wang looked, the surer he felt that it really was his father.

It was near midnight when the white-robed genie cried, "Why not use this beautiful moonlight to enjoy a game of football?"

"Good idea!" cried the other two. The youngest servant dove into the water. He quickly reappeared with a brilliant crystal football. The three genies stood, and the one in white shouted, "Old man, kick off!"

The fifth servant placed the ball on the net and gave it a mighty kick. The shining ball rose high into the air. It rose so high and traveled so fast it seemed to be a streak of silver drawn across the night sky. For a moment one might have

thought the ball would never come down. Then it plunged earthward and landed with a thunderous crash on the deck of Wang's junk.

Wang felt himself being overcome by his love for the game. Without thinking, he kicked the ball off again with all his might. It soared across the sky like a comet, leaving a bright trail, then fell into the lake with a splash. It bobbed up for a moment, spun around, then sank for good.

"Who did that?" shouted the genies. "Who dares interfere with our game?"

The old servant, however, could not contain his enthusiasm. He applauded and shouted, "Hurray! Well played! That's the 'comet-kick,' a trick known only by men of my family."

"Silence, old fool!" cried the genie in white. He clapped his hands and called for the youngest servant. "You and the old man go and bring me the one who lost our ball and spoiled the game. If you return without him, beware!"

Wang and his crew heard all plainly. The terrified sailors scurried for shelter. As for Wang, he calmly drew his saber, stood proudly in view on deck, and waited. As the old man and the boy approached, walking upon the lake in the reflection of the moon, Wang knew without a doubt that the old servant was his father. Full of joy and emotion, he shouted as loud as he could, "Father, it is me, Wang, your son!"

"Fly for your life as fast as you can, son!" shouted the brave old man. "If you do not, they will capture and kill you!"

Hearing these words, the young servant looked from the old man to the son on the junk. Then he turned around, and dove into the water. He clearly wanted no part in this strange encounter.

At this moment, the three genies rose from their net and came swiftly toward Wang's junk. They were furious and their eyes flashed lightning. They rushed at the old man just as he began to clamber aboard the junk, and seized him. Wang ran at them brandishing his saber.

A tremendous fight followed, the fury of which tipped the junk to the side and broke the cable that anchored it. As soon as this happened the current took the junk and pulled it faster and faster over the black water.

Wang had managed to grab the robe of one of the genies in yellow, and had freed his father. During all the confusion, the attackers had dived overboard and vanished into the lake. Wang was left holding the yellow robe.

He dropped it to the deck and ran to the side of the junk to see what had happened. The net, the banquet, and the four servants had entirely disappeared. Not far from the junk, a storm was brewing. The wind got stronger and stronger until the water became so rough that huge waves crashed with the frightening noise of an avalanche. The other boats that were on the lake that night were wrecked. But Wang, who rallied his frightened crew, and ordered them to row for shore with all their might, saved his junk.

Finally, when the lake had calmed and they were nearly home, Wang embraced his father and questioned him. "Tell me what happened. Where have you been these eight years?"

His father stretched, breathing deeply and smiling for joy. "I was never drowned at all," he told Wang. "Those lake genies snatched me off the deck and dragged me down to the bottom of the lake with them for one reason only. They wanted me to teach them how to play football. They could never get to see a game, because they only can take human form and come to the surface at night when the moon is full. The rest of the time they are nothing but fish. You freed me from them tonight, my boy. Now I can come home to live with you and be merry again for the rest of my days."

As the first rays of the morning sun appeared in the sky, Wang said, "Never will I get another chance to kick a crystal ball, and that's a good thing. It makes a fine appearance, all silver against the sky, but it is hard on the foot."

Just then the junk reached shore. As they were about to leave it, Wang's father turned, and pointed at the deck.

Wang followed the direction of his father's hand with his eyes, and gave a cry of surprise. For there, where he had dropped the yellow robe, lay the bony skeleton of a big fish.

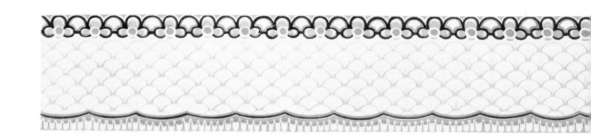

HUANG AND THE THUNDER GENIE

The villagers all said Huang was the most generous young man alive. They all cited examples of his generosity to justify their opinion. If Huang overheard them, he frowned and shook his head. For he was very modest and thought he did no more than his duty. But the villagers talked on, since nothing pleased them more than friendly gossip.

When his friend Si-A died penniless, Huang thought it only natural that he should take on the responsibility for Si-A's mother and six young brothers. Since he was a scholar and had never worked, his small fortune was soon eaten up by the excellent appetites of Si-A's family.

"This can't go on. I'll have to do something," Huang thought. "While I spend my time writing and reading delightful books, that poor family goes hungry. It's time for me to try my hand at accounts rather than verses."

The villagers were thrilled by Huang's noble sacrifice. They readily came to buy from him when he opened up his shop. His business prospered and Huang the poor student quickly became Huang the wealthy merchant.

One day, coming home from a buying trip in Nanking, he stopped to rest at an inn. He was about to drink a cup of tea when a very tall man came in, who was so thin he seemed all bones and resembled a skeleton. He went to a corner and sat with his head in his hands. Huang was touched. He went over to the stranger and asked if he might be of help. The thin man shook his head and said nothing. But when dinner was served, Huang silently set a full plate before the stranger. The man set to work and consumed the food ravenously. "Would you like more, my friend?" Huang asked. Without waiting for a reply, he ordered a complete meal for two and had it served to the man, who ate it all in several minutes. After this, Huang ordered a large roast and a dozen loaves of bread. The man ate them, too, as soon as they were served.

When he had eaten his fill, he turned to thank Huang. "It has been three years since I last satisfied my hunger," he explained.

Huang didn't know what to make of that. "May I ask who you are, sir, and where you come from?" he murmured.

"Sir, I'm sorry, but I may not tell you my name. As for my address, I can only say that I live neither on the earth in a house nor on the water in a boat."

Huang was confused. But he smiled politely, since it was clearly useless to ask further. He sent for his baggage and started to leave. To his astonishment, the tall stranger followed him.

"Sir, there is no reason for you to come with me," Huang said.

"You are in grave danger," said the man. "I cannot forget your kindness and leave you alone to endure it."

Huang protested no more and soon got used to the idea of having a traveling companion.

The next time they stopped for refreshment, he would have ordered another huge meal for the two of them. But the stranger said, "Nothing for me, thank you. I eat only once a year."

By now Huang was no longer surprised, and did not insist. He had guessed his companion must be a genie. Huang felt the suitable thing to do was to enjoy the honor of the genie's company, mind his own manners, and ask no questions.

46

Next day they were crossing a river on a junk, when a sudden, violent wind tipped and sank the boat and all its passengers. Huang and his companion and all Huang's goods were plunged into the water. Huang managed to stay afloat. When the brief storm was over, the tall man took Huang on his back and swam with him to a junk the storm had spared. He put Huang aboard, then dove underwater. Huang sat on the deck, too dazed to move.

The tall man soon reappeared, carrying an armload of Huang's baggage, which he tossed onto the junk. Then he dove again. Huang was examining the first bundle when the man added another armload to the pile, and dove once more. He went down again and again until every one of Huang's bags, baskets, and bundles had been retrieved.

Huang did not quite know how to express his gratitude. He exclaimed, "I owe you everything. First you save my life, then you save all my worldly goods!"

47

The man answered, "Now there is no further reason for me to come with you. We can say farewell if you like."

"Please!" Huang exclaimed. "Stay with me. Let us finish this voyage together. Perhaps you'll help me get these things back in order."

The man seemed pleased. He gladly came aboard and helped sort out the collection of goods which had scarcely had time to get wet. At last, Huang said, "Imagine! On a crossing where so many lost their lives, I lost nothing but one gold hairpin!"

He was horrified to see the stranger dive under the water for perhaps the twentieth time that day. In a few seconds, the man rose, holding out a gold hairpin. "There," he said. "I was lucky. I found it at once and was able to do you another service."

This final stroke of kindness left Huang speechless for a moment. When he could speak, he said, "If you have neither house nor boat, why don't you come stay permanently with me?"

The tall man gladly agreed. They lived together in Huang's house, and became the best of friends.

Twelve months after he first met his guest at the inn, Huang secretly ordered enough of the best food for a great banquet. He had recalled that his friend ate but once a year. Sure enough, the banquet prepared for a hundred men just nicely satisfied the tall man's appetite. "I never met anyone like you," he said to Huang warmly as he finished the last crumb. "You are truly unusual. You think constantly of others, never of yourself."

Huang frowned and shook his head. He felt he had done nothing worthy of praise. The tall man went on, "I must soon leave you for good. Now I can tell you who I am, if you like. I am the Thunder Genie. I was punished for certain foolish acts by having to spend five years on earth. The five years are almost over."

At this news, Huang, awed and respectful, asked the genie to forgive him for having only an ordinary house and not a palace, in which to entertain his guest.

But the Thunder Genie scolded him for apologizing. "You know I have been happy here. Now, if you have a wish, tell me. I shall see that it is fulfilled."

A peal of thunder sounded in the distance. Huang seeing a cloud drift across the heavens, got an idea. "How I should like to travel among the clouds!" he said.

The genie laughed. He laughed still more when Huang, seconds later, balanced himself on the tip of a cloud high in the air. Huang was awestruck and terribly afraid as he looked up at the heavens. The sky studded with stars looked like a diamond crown. He held out his arms towards the brightness, and a star tumbled down into his sleeve.

Suddenly two dragons appeared, drawing a carriage. Their swinging tails made a sound like the cracking of a whip on a cymbal. Within the carriage was a huge vat of water and a most beautiful fairy who seemed to be watching over it. A dozen genies followed after the carriage. Among them Huang recognized his friend the Thunder Genie.

The Thunder Genie came up to him. Smiling, he took Huang by the hand, and pointing to the fairy, said, "That is the Rain Fairy. She is so provoked by the silliness of mankind that she is punishing the countryside with a long dry spell."

Then he presented Huang to the lovely lady, saying, "This is my good friend."

The lovely fairy smiled graciously and motioned to Huang to take one of the pails that hung along the outside of her carriage. He obeyed, then looked to the Thunder Genie for an explanation. The genie made a gesture, and the clouds parted. Huang could see for miles. Below lay his native village, in the heart of the drought-parched land. He understood what he was supposed to do. He filled the pail with water from the vat, and tossed it down. The Rain Fairy didn't try to stop him. She continued to smile, so he tossed down more.

The Thunder Genie said, "Now you may return to earth. Take hold of the rope behind the carriage, and relax. There is nothing to fear."

Huang was afraid, but knew he could trust the genie. He gripped the rope and began to slide down it. Suddenly he found himself right in his own room, as if he had never left it.

When he went out of his house, the villagers seemed particularly happy. A friend said to him, "What luck to have had that wonderful, unexpected rain storm! Now our crops are safe for this year."

Huang knew why the rain had fallen, though he kept silent. Nobody else seemed to realize that Huang was responsible.

That night as he was getting ready for bed, a black stone dropped from his sleeve. He picked it up and remembered the star that had fallen when he visited the sky. The stone was dark and cold, but he set it on his table, as a most precious souvenir.

During the night something woke him. On his table the star blazed brightly and lit up his whole room. He rose and went toward it. As he reached the table, the star lengthened and changed and became a beautiful maiden who looked at him with great sweetness. "My lord, I am Bright Cloud," she said in a musical voice. "The Thunder Genie has sent me to be your wife."

Huang was beside himself with joy. He summoned his servants, sent for his family and friends, and ordered a wedding banquet.

During the ceremony, thunder rumbled overhead and a light rain dashed briefly down. The glad bridal pair bowed, for they knew that their friends high in the clouds, were sending them their blessings.

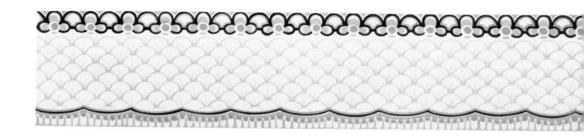

TAO'S DREAM

In a village near Nanking lived a young man who was admired by everyone for his learning and his goodness. Tao was his name. Those in need of help or advice could always count on his wisdom and generosity.

One night as he slept, he felt someone shake his arm. When he opened his eyes, he saw a man dressed in gray standing beside his bed, looking anxiously at him.

"Who are you?" Tao exclaimed.

"My mistress requests that you come to see her."

"And who is your mistress?"

"She lives not far from here," was the man's only answer.

Intrigued, Tao dressed and went with the man in gray. They circled Tao's house a few times, and Tao suddenly found himself in a place that he was sure he had never seen before. The houses were strangely shaped. They were all right next to one another, and had many doors. Crowds of ladies and gentlemen hurried here and there, in all directions. Whenever one passed the man in gray he asked, "Is my lord Tao here yet?"

The man simply nodded.

All this did not fail to arouse Tao's curiosity. Wishing to know what was happening to him, he finally said to his guide, "I have never had the honor of meeting you before, and this place is strange to me. You must understand that I am getting suspicious. Who is your mistress and where are we going?"

"My mistress is waiting impatiently to meet you," replied the man. "She knows you to be a person of excellent family and great wisdom, a man of whom all speak with respect. Soon you will see her for yourself." Tao knew that it was futile to question this man any further.

Suddenly, two maidens with banners of embroidered silk appeared. They placed themselves on either side of Tao and led him into a room where a regal woman sat enthroned on a raised dais.

She rose and came down the steps to welcome her guest. Tao was too impressed to ask any questions. The queen, for indeed, that is what she was, said simply, "I have the good fortune to be a neighbor of yours. Please do not be nervous and make yourself comfortable."

She made a brief sign to her maidens, and they approached, bringing goblets of the most exquisite drink Tao had ever tasted. He drank several glasses full. Then the queen spoke again. "My lord Tao, I have a daughter whose name is Lotus Flower. She is beautiful and very young. I should like you to meet her."

She clapped her hands and said to one of her maidens, "Ask the princess to come here at once."

Several minutes later, the sound of footsteps were heard, and a floral fragrance drifted into the room. The princess entered. "My lord Tao, this is my daughter, Lotus Flower," said the queen.

Tao was struck by the young girl's beauty. But before he could pay her a compliment, he was interrupted by a lady of the court who ran crying, "The monster has broken into the palace!"

Tao got up quickly. He was not afraid. But he did not know what to expect, and

he wanted to be prepared. The queen seized his hand and said in a trembling voice, "I beg of you, do not abandon us. My whole kingdom is in danger. You are my last hope. Please read this message."

She handed him a paper which he unrolled and read. The message said this: "I, Black Wing, Your Majesty's obedient subject, beg you to move your capital at once in order to save the lives of your people. A monstrous serpent thousands of yards long is nearing the Gold Gate. He has already attacked many of Your Majesty's devoted subjects so that villages have become deserts. His head is as big as a mountain, and he can swallow a whole house in one gulp. I, Black Wing, humbly pray that Your Majesty will flee with the royal family before it is too late."

Tao, having finished this message, turned pale. The queen said to him, "Now do you understand why I have summoned you and why I need your help?"

53

"Yes I do, Your Majesty," replied Tao. "But isn't it too late? The monster is already in your palace."

"Save my daughter, Lotus Flower," said the queen. "I entrust you with her life."

Tao turned towards the princess and took her hand. She looked up through her tears and asked in a tiny voice, "Where are you taking me?"

That, indeed, was a good question. Tao thought a minute and then said simply, "I am only a poor young man. I am sorry to say that I do not have a beautiful house. I can only offer you a few bare rooms. But my poor home is much safer now than this royal palace. Will you come with me?"

"I see that I must," Lotus Flower sobbed. "Let's go quickly."

Tao ran with her, out of the palace, out of the town, and up to his own modest house. Once inside, Lotus Flower looked around her and said, "This is indeed a house in which peace and safety can be found. Now that I have obeyed and followed you, will you do as I ask?"

"I will, if I can," Tao said.

"Then build a new capital and a new palace, so that my relatives and subjects may come and live in peace."

"How can I?" Tao groaned. "I haven't the means to build so much as a summer house in my garden."

"Oh, my lord Tao," cried the princess amid her tears, "why then do you have so great a reputation for helping your neighbors when they need you?"

Tao hardly knew what to reply. She wept, and he tried desperately to console her.

Suddenly he woke and found himself sitting up in bed. "So it was a dream!" he exclaimed. However, a faint sound of human sorrowing continued to sound in his ears. "Or was it?" he wondered.

He looked around him and saw a few bees buzzing in the room, near the window. He had just noticed them, when his best friend came in. "What's the matter? You have never looked so puzzled," said his friend.

"I will tell you a strange dream I had tonight," replied Tao.

Tao told him the whole dream and described the way Lotus Flower's grieving had changed into the gentle buzzing of bees.

His friend was astonished. He approached the bees near the window and tried to chase them away. They did not fly away frightened as insects usually do, but remained in the room. "Tao," his friend said, "whatever the dream meant, everyone knows that bees are a symbol of plenty. Why not build a hive for these? They obviously don't have one to go to."

Tao followed his advice and began to work on a hive. No sooner was it ready than a swarm of bees flew in. There were so many bees in this swarm that, for a moment, the sky seemed to be covered by a golden cloud.

"I wonder where they came from," thought Tao. After visiting several neighbors in his village who kept bees, he found the answer. An old gentleman who lived nearby led him into the middle of his garden where he had a hive. All was silent. The old man lifted the top of the hive, and he and Tao saw a fat snake coiled inside. The snake seemed to be sleeping off a heavy meal.

"That's the monster in my dream!" Tao shouted. "My bees came to me from your hive!"

The old gentleman nodded, smiling. "It seems to me a good omen, Tao. Keep the bees. They came to you for help, and you sheltered them. They will bring you good luck. May you and they prosper!"

Prosper they did. The bees living in Tao's hive became more and more numerous. Soon his garden was ringed with hives all rich with honey. And from the bees' industrious and orderly villages, came a gentle murmuring which soothed Tao during his working and sleeping hours.

THE EXTRAORDINARY BEGGAR

An excellent, young doctor lived in Kuang Li. Everyone admired him for his skill and for his good heart. The Provincial Governor himself was his friend and often asked his advice on government affairs. The doctor, whose name was Kao, took care of rich and poor alike. He was even known to treat patients who could pay nothing at all.

One day an old beggar staggered into the village, his body covered with festering wounds. He was so disgusting that no one would go near him, and he lay in the street, without even the energy to moan or cry out. There he would surely have died, but Kao happened to pass and see him. He called his two servants immediately, and had them put the beggar to bed in a quiet little room that opened onto the courtyard of his home. Reluctantly, the servants obeyed, for their master expected obedience. The beggar looked as though he could not live through the night.

Kao worked over him, using all his skill, applying all the latest medications. That night and the next he watched by his patient's bedside.

Slowly the wounds healed and the beggar began to show signs of life. Several days passed. Suddenly one day, the sick man opened his eyes. He commanded the servants, "Bring me soup and bread at once!"

The servants were shocked at his impudence. They hurried to tell their master that the beggar had dared to give them orders.

"Good, good!" exclaimed Kao with pleasure. "Give him plenty of rich, hot soup with all the bread he can eat. And be quick about it!"

The servants bowed their heads and obeyed.

The next day, the beggar sat up in bed and commanded in a loud voice, "Bring me meat and wine!"

The servants were even more shocked. They raced to Kao to complain once again.

But, as before, Kao seemed pleased. "Splendid, splendid!" he said. "Give him plenty of good rare meat and a flagon of the best wine. And be quick about it!"

The servants obeyed. But they despised the beggar who did not beg, and did not even thank them for doing their duty. On the contrary, as he regained his strength he demanded more and more attention, just as if he were not an old beggar but a person of authority.

The next time Kao visited the guest room, the invalid, stiff and sore though he was, rose to bow deeply to Kao. "I am extremely grateful to you, doctor," he said. "Death had already laid a hand on me, when you appeared and gave me back my life. Some day, I hope, I will be able to show you that I am not ungrateful."

"You are too good, my friend. I am well repaid by seeing you healed," said Kao smiling. "Let me counsel you, however, to stay awhile longer with me. Your strength has barely begun to return."

Kao felt a strange liking for the old beggar. He wished they might be friends for the rest of their lives and be near each other always. For the moment, he simply instructed his servants to treat the old man with as much honor as they would have shown a visiting prince.

The servants took this with bad humor. They resented taking orders from a mere beggar, especially one whose sharp eyes seemed to see everything. For whenever they tried to shirk their work, he caught them.

Together the servants planned a horrible revenge. Late one night, as everyone slept, they set fire to the guest room. They waited until tall flames leaped from it before giving the alarm.

Kao ran to the little room only to find it entirely aflame. "My poor friend is surely dead in that furnace," he wept. With the hope of at least recovering the body, he approached the blaze.

There amid the flames, untouched and sleeping peacefully, lay the old man. Kao's cry of astonishment woke him. He opened his eyes, peered through the fire at Kao, and asked lightly, "What on earth has happened to your guest room?"

It was then that Kao and his servants guessed that the patient must be a magician. Kao bowed low out of respect. His servants bowed too, then quickly took to their heels for fear they would be punished.

But the servants were beneath the old man's notice. He helped Kao rise, and said, "My name is Wu, and I am a magician. I have been given a span of time to live on earth, and to run the risks of mortal men. When you found me, robbers had stolen all I owned and beaten me till they thought me dead."

"Since the robbers took all you had, great Wu, be kind and stay with me. Your companionship is a rare pleasure."

"I have just a little more time to pass on earth. It will be delightful to spend it with you."

So Wu lived in Kao's house. Kao provided him with the finest robes he had, and did his best to be a good host. They had long talks together, often over a game of dominoes. Kao learned much from his wise and eminent guest.

But finally, a day came when the magician said, "My time has run out. I must take leave of you. May I thank you for your kindness by offering you a farewell banquet?"

Sadly Kao replied, "I have had such pleasure in your company. Can't you stay? At any rate, you mustn't go to the trouble of preparing a feast."

Wu smiled. "It is no trouble at all. There will be just the two of us, here in your garden."

"In my garden?" Kao asked. Kao's garden was just big enough to hold a tiny summer house with two benches. It didn't seem to be a place for banquets. Besides, it was winter. The trees were bare, and it was so cold a man could freeze his nose by putting it out of doors to smell the wind.

"You will see," said Wu. "Follow me." He led the way out to the center of the garden. As he approached the summer house, Kao felt the air change. It seemed suddenly like spring. Following Wu inside, Kao gasped with surprise.

The summer house was ten times bigger than usual, and contained ebony furniture set with carved jade. Beside a table, stood a folding screen made of rock crystal. It was decorated with a flowering tree that seemed to move gently in the breeze. Petals floated slowly down from its branches to the base of the screen. In its topmost twigs a bird sang.

60

Kao reached toward the screen. He tried to touch the tree and the bird. But when his hand was close enough, they disappeared and the screen reflected only his outstretched fingers. It was a delightful invention.

"Serve the tea!" ordered Wu, clapping his hands.

At once a sun appeared on the screen. From the middle of it flew a phoenix, the immortal firebird that rises anew from its own ashes. It carried, balanced on its beak, a tray upon which were two cups of exquisitely fragrant tea. The phoenix waited motionless until Kao and Wu had finished drinking and had replaced their cups. Then it took the tray in its beak and flew back into the sun.

"Serve the dinner!" ordered Wu, clapping his hands.

From the sun on the screen flew a brilliant green phoenix and a golden crane who busily set about putting bowls and napkins on the table. Assisted by four multicolored birds, they came and went many times setting dozens of dishes of exotic food before Kao and Wu.

After they had eaten, Wu said, "I should now like you to try the wine that only magicians may drink. For this occasion, it is also poured for you."

He clapped his hands again; the screen glittered, and from the sun flew an enormous butterfly. Its wings contained all the colors of the rainbow and were spotted with gold and silver. It carried a mother-of-pearl shell full of amber wine.

"Butterfly, pour the wine," said Wu.

Immediately the butterfly became a stately young girl clothed in robes the color of the butterfly's wings. She approached with dignity and filled their crystal glasses from her shell. Then she bowed, and once more became a butterfly that flew off and disappeared into the sun.

Kao was speechless. All these extraordinary wonders made him feel as if he must be dreaming. It seemed to him that Wu's wise, smiling face was at the center of the dream. He no longer knew where he was. He shook his head to clear it. Wu took his arm and helped him out of the summer house.

Breathing deeply of the cold night air, Kao wondered if he had, perhaps, dreamed it all. Maybe Wu was only the poor beggar he had found dying in the road. A high moon stood silver in the sky. It gave Kao an idea of how to test Wu's power.

"Surely no man has ever before enjoyed a banquet as sumptuous and full of delights as this one you have given me," he said. "You are certainly a magician of great power. Is it within your power to let me have a close look at the glories of the sky?"

"Nothing could be simpler," Wu replied, taking his hand. They soared up, higher and higher, until Kao was so frightened, he no longer dared look down. Instead, he stared upward, and high above he saw a great stone gateway whose summit was round as a well.

When they went through the gateway, they were dazzled by a blinding silver light that bathed in brilliance a stairway and a path paved with blue, lustrous stones like pearls.

At the foot of the stairs rose a tall tree covered with red lotus blossoms. Beneath this tree sat a maiden in robes of deep scarlet, playing a strange and haunting tune on her lute.

Wide-eyed, Kao stared at the young girl and listened to her song. As soon as the maiden saw him, she cried, "What brings a mortal man to this place?"

Wu whispered to Kao, "Many sprites and genies cannot tolerate mortals."

He led Kao from the gate to a snowy cloud bank and he said, "Friend, farewell. We must leave each other. I have reached my home. My span of time on earth is over." Kao was overcome with emotion. He wanted to thank Wu, but Wu went on quickly, "Listen to this final word, and remember it well. You will find yourself in danger of death. Tomorrow, very early, flee to the hills in the west. This is your only hope. Otherwise you are lost."

Kao wished for a more detailed explanation but there was no time to lose. The cloud bank where he stood began to move. It descended quickly in vast circles that grew narrower as it neared earth. Soon Kao found himself back in his own tiny garden.

When he went into his house, he told his wife the story, for he could not keep it to himself.

"I agree that it may have been a dream," she said sweetly. "But my dear lord, perhaps the warning is true. I don't know if you have really toured the skies. However, the old man was certainly real, and was a real magician, for he has vanished. You can lose nothing by taking his advice. At worst, you will have a day's rest, which will do you good because you work so hard."

Kao nodded in agreement. Her loving words were full of good sense.

Very early the next day he slung a double sack of provisions over his shoulder and began walking toward the western hills. It was snowing so heavily that it was difficult for him to follow the road. He struck out across country, always keeping west. Something urged him to hurry, hurry.

He tried to watch his step, but all at once he slipped and went over the edge of a deep ravine. He slid down farther and farther, until he found himself shaken but unhurt at the bottom. Kao had no idea how far he had fallen. He looked for a way out, and saw that the top of the ravine was now covered by a cloud that looked almost like a lid.

Kao sighed, and said to himself, "Wu advised me to hurry to the western hills and hide myself, but here I am. How can I get out of this impossible pit?" Very sadly, he sat down on the floor of the ravine and thought about his adventure.

Snow no longer dazzled his eyes, and his sight cleared. Suddenly he saw a light that seemed to be coming from a crack in the steep wall. Kao followed the light and pushed his way through the crack. He immediately found himself in an immense room with vast painted walls. It was empty, save for three old men sitting in the middle at an ebony table, playing dominoes.

They glanced up as Kao entered. But they showed no interest in his presence. Since no one gave him a greeting, Kao made himself small in a corner and sat watching the game.

Finally, the game was over. The players replaced the dominoes in a box of ebony and mother-of-pearl and turned, at last, to Kao.

"How in the world did you get here?" one of the three asked.

Kao answered simply, "I was walking through the snow when I slipped and fell down the side of the ravine."

A second of the three said, "This is no place for a mortal man. It is not fitting for you to stay long with us."

The third old man rose and took Kao's hand. "Come, I shall see that you get safely home," he said, leading Kao outside.

Upon leaving the room, they came to the bottom of the ravine where Kao had first found himself.

Kao looked up, and saw that the cloud which had covered the ravine was descending toward him. The old man gestured courteously, and Kao climbed onto the cloud. It rose, and very soon Kao was above ground again, standing on a hill.

Amazed, Kao looked around him. The trees on the hill tossed in an autumn wind, scattering golden leaves upon the earth. "When I left here this morning it was winter. Now it has become autumn. What has happened?" he demanded loudly of the empty air. He ran down the hill and all the way home, arriving at his house quite out of breath.

66

When his wife saw him, she flung herself, weeping, into his arms. "Why are you crying?" he asked. "Here I am safe and sound, and I have only been gone since dawn."

"That dawn was ages ago. You have been gone for almost three years!" she cried. "I thought you were dead and gone forever."

Bewildered, Kao said to himself, "It seemed like only a few hours. Could it really have been three years?" Then, turning toward his wife, he asked, "Tell me, what has happened since I left?"

"Dreadful things," she replied tearfully. "An enemy of your good friend the governor lied to the emperor about him and ruined his career. Everything was taken from him, and all his friends were put to death or imprisoned. The very day you left, two soldiers came to arrest you for treason. They hunted you in the hills for two long years."

"What about now? Am I still a wanted man?"

"Now all is well again. Your good friend the governor has proven his innocence, and the emperor is kinder to him than ever before."

"Then Wu's advice saved me," Kao said.

Kao went back to work caring for the villagers, who loved him for his kindness and respected him for his medical skill. Once in a while he would sit in the tiny summer house in the center of his garden and think of the banquet that Wu had made for him and the marvels he had seen that memorable night. It was a pleasant memory, but so extraordinary that the details escaped him. All he could clearly recall was the wise and benevolent face of his friend, Wu.

ABCDEFGH